NEWSPAPER ADVERTISING WORKBOOK

For
Wild Bird Speciality Stores

Book 3 of the NAIWBS Marketing Brief Series

Published by
NAIWBS

TABLE OF CONTENTS:

While this booklet was designed for Wild Bird Speciality stores it can be used as a guide for any Retail Store

---

ADVERTISING:

Building a relationship with your customer

To be successful in business and in your advertising efforts you must establish a relationship with your customer that is more than store owner - customer. The relationship you build must be based on you knowing your customer needs and wants, then providing the product or service that meets that want or need. Without a sound relationship with your customer you cannot and you will not succeed.

Consequently advertising is one of the most important and exciting aspects of running your wild bird store. It is by no means the only one, but it is an important one. It is absolutely necessary to advertise and promote, in order to get your name out to the public and keep your sales growing. In addition, advertising lets you utilize the creative side of your business skill to compete with your competitors for those all important buyers.

There are three things to remember when advertising:

First: Your advertisements and promotions must be designed to get customers into your store and then to buy your products.

Second: Make sure your advertisements are interesting, enthusiastic and easy to understand.

Third: Advertising requires a long term commitment. It is not something you do now and then. You must budget for advertising and then advertise and advertise and advertise again. *

Seth Godin in the Guerrilla Marketing Handbook tells us that 'on average only one out of nine well designed ads is ever seen by the targeted customer. We also know that an ad needs to be seen at least three times before it make enough of an impact to spur action.   If that isn't a sound reason for continual advertising I don't know what is.

Remember
Three or more times
before it makes an impact

NEWSPAPER ADVERTISING

Currently, newspaper is the most common form of advertising used by Wild Bird Stores, while cable TV is a strong second. Most stores use newspaper advertising for four reasons. First: Most areas have a newspaper that services the people in the stores local market. Second: Newspapers tend to be the most affordable mass media available to Wild Bird Stores and all small business. Third: Newspaper ads are easy to prepare and can change from week to week, making it easy to adapt to the store owners advertising goals. Fourth: Newspapers generally produce good response if the advertising is done on a consistent basis.

If you choose to advertise in a newspaper, we recommend that it be a "daily". This does not mean that you have to advertise every day of the week. Many Wild Bird Stores will run only one ad per week.

When you advertise in a daily paper you should try getting your ads placed in a section that will be read by the people most likely to be your customers. The first section that we would recommend would be the main news section of the paper. Pages 2 or 3 would be preferable. However, the option of picking your page is not always possible because many newspapers have a 'run of the paper' policy meaning that your ad will be placed wherever the editor wants. In some newspapers it is possible to guarantee a page, but the paper will generally charge you extra for that location. We have some stores who feel very strongly that 'paid position' is worth the extra money.

Your second location option is to try to be in a newspaper section where the articles being read relate in some way to the backyard birding business. The idea being that if the person is interested enough to read the articles in this section, they will also be interested enough to read the ads which cater to these same interests. In the case of Wild Bird Stores these sections tend to be either "Out-door" or "Gardening". Generally these sections will only run once a week.

If your store is located in a large metropolitan area you generally will not be able to afford to or want to advertise in the main daily paper unless it offers regional distribution. Some newspapers will have a regional insert section that is focused at one micro area of a large city. This insert allows the newspaper to report on stories that might be of interest in one part of the city but not another. The section also allows a small business to focus its advertising in the local community at an affordable price. Wild Bird Stores who have consistently advertised in this type of section have had good results.

In contrast, stores that are in more rural areas may only have access to weekly papers. In this case you will want to combine your advertising with other mediums.

*(**A special note of warning:** If you are going to advertise in a weekly newspaper make sure that it is more than an advertising publication. By this we mean, make sure that more space is dedicated to the articles rather than the advertisements.)*

CHECKLIST FOR SETTING ADVERTISING BUDGETS

Begin by setting a sales goal

Write down the estimated sales figures for each month of the current year. Then, in view of your own knowledge and judgment of this year's picture, rough in sales goals for the coming twelve months. Remember - No goals, No glory.

Decide How Much Advertising

Considering your planned sales goal. What your competition is likely to do. Then write in your planned advertising budget for the coming year. (See next section) The following profit pointers can be used to double-check your own thinking on the advertising budget you can afford and need to do the job:

☐ Stores in less favorable locations advertise more.

☐ So do those that are new and expanding.

☐ Strong competition raises the size of the budget needed.

☐ Special dates and events offer additional sales opportunities.

☐ Taking advantage of co-op support can stretch ad dollars and increase ad frequency.

Decide What to Promote

As your business grows let your business experience guide you in weighing the advertising you will invest in each of your product categories each month. For instance, if the sales goal of feeders is 9 percent of the total store sales objective this month, then earmark for it something like 9 percent of the month's planned advertising space. Your list shouldn't be a straightjacket, but a basic outline. Use the following list to help you decide what to promote:

- ❑ Check the month's heavy traffic pullers.

- ❑ Look for products whose seasonal curve drops next month and should be cleared.

- ❑ Promote newly expanded product lines harder.

- ❑ Calculate co-op support available for each manufacturers line.

Make a Schedule

For each month, fill in a schedule to take full advantage of

- ❑ Payroll days of important firms in your area.

- ❑ Days of the week traffic is heaviest in your center or store.

- ❑ National and local merchandising events offering tie-in possibilities. For example, February is "National Bird Feeding Month".

- ❑ New or expanded product categories.

- ❑ Current prices and your stock on hand—jot down items, prices, and ad sizes for each ad.

THE ADVERTISING BUDGET:

You will want to run your advertising budget on a "Percent of Monthly sales" system. To do this you will have to estimate your monthly sales figures for the coming twelve months. For purposes of this demonstration we will assume gross sales of $ 200,000. for the coming year. We will set our advertising budget at 10 percent of gross sales. Therefore our annual advertising budget is $ 20,000.

Jan.	Feb.	Mar	Apr.	May	Jun.	Jul.	Aug.
0.05	0.04	0.06	0.07	0.09	0.09	0.07	0.07

Sept.	Oct.	Nov.	Dec.
0.07	0.07	0.10	0.21

These figurers are estimates, use numbers
from your store's history.

Next using the monthly percentages shown above multiply $20,000 by the monthly number. This gives you your monthly advertising budget. Do this for each month.

Because some months are very low and others very high, we suggest you take one third of your highest two months advertising budget and allocate it to the lowest two months advertising budget. This will then provide you with and adequate monthly advertising budget.

TEN REASONS TO ADVERTISE:

1. You must advertise to reach new customers.
Your market changes constantly. The shopper who wouldn't consider your business a few years ago may be a prime customer today. Remember on average your customers move every three years.

2. You must advertise continuously.
Shoppers don't have the store loyalty they once did. Shoppers have mobility and freedom of choice. Stores must promote to get former customers to return and to seek new ones.

3. You must advertise to remain with shoppers through the buying process.
Many people often go from store to store to compare prices, quality and service. Advertising must reach them steadily through the entire decision making process.

4. You must advertise because your competition is advertising.
There are only so many consumers in the market ready to buy at any one time. You have got to advertise to keep regular customers, and to counterbalance the advertising of your competitors.

5. You must advertise to make your business grow.
A survey of more than 3,000 companies found that Advertisers who maintained or expanded advertising over a five-year period saw their sales increase an average of 100%. Companies who cut advertising averaged sales increases of 45% .

6. You must advertise to generate store traffic.
Continuous store traffic is the first step toward sales increases and expanding your base of shoppers.

7. You must advertise to make more sales.
Advertising works. Businesses that succeed are usually strong, steady advertisers.

8. You must advertise because there is always business to generate.
As long as you're in business, you've got overhead to meet, and new people to reach. Advertising can generate customers now and in the future.

9. You must advertise to keep a healthy positive image.
In a competitive market, rumors and bad news travels fast. Advertising that is vigorous and positive can bring shopper into your store, regardless of the economy.

10. You must advertise because it takes seven exposures before a customer responds.
 Research shows that a customer must be exposed to your store and its products at least seven different times before that customer finally buys something. Now you know why your existing customer base is so important. It cost lots of money to get a customer ($7 to $ 10), but a little care, concern and contact is all that it takes to keep a customer.

CHECKLIST FOR CREATING NEWSPAPER ADVERTISING

Make your ads easily recognizable. Studies have shown that advertisements that are distinctive in their use of art, layout techniques, and typefaces usually enjoy a higher readership than run-of-the mill advertising. Try to make your ads distinctively different in appearance from the advertising of your competitors— and then keep your ads' appearance consistent. This way, readers will recognize your ads even before they read them.

Use a simple layout. Ads should not be crossword puzzles. The layout should carry the reader's eye through the message easily and in proper sequence from headline, to illustration, to explanatory copy, to price, to your store's name. Avoid the use of too many different typefaces, overly decorative borders, and reverses (white on black).

Use a dominant element in large picture or headline to ensure quick visibility. Photographs and realistic drawings have about equal attention-getting value, but photographs of real people and action pictures win more readership. Photographs of local people or places also have high attention value. Color increases the number of readers.

Use a prominent benefit headline. The first question a reader asks of an ad is: "What's in it for me?" Select the main benefit that your merchandise offers and feature it in a compelling headline. Amplify this message in subheads.

Avoid generalized quality claims. Your headline will be easier to read if it is black on white and is not printed on part of the illustration.

Let your white space work for you. Don't overcrowd your ad. White space is an important layout element in newspaper advertising because the average page is so heavy with small type. White space focuses the reader's attention on your ad and will make your headline and illustration stand out. When a "crowded" ad is necessary, such as for a sale, departmentalize your items so that the reader can find his or her way through them easily.

Make your copy complete. Know all there is to know about the merchandise you sell and select the benefits most appealing to your customers. These benefits might have to do with fashion, design, performance, or the construction of your merchandise. Sizes and colors available are important, pertinent information.

State price or range of prices. Dollar figures have good attention value. Don't be afraid to quote your price, even if it's high. Readers often will overestimate omitted prices. If the advertised price is high, explain why the item represents a good value- perhaps because of superior materials or workmanship or extra luxury features. Point out the actual savings to the reader and spell out layaway plans.

Specify brand name merchandise. If the item is a known brand, say so in your advertising. Manufacturers spend large sums to sell their goods, and you can capitalize on their advertising while enhancing the reputation of your store by featuring brand name items.

Include related items. Make two sales instead of one by offering related items along with a featured one. For Instance, when a feeder is advertised, also show a bag of seed.

Urge your readers to buy now. Ask for the sale. You can stimulate prompt action by using such phrases as "limited supply" or "this week only." If mail-order coupons are included in your ads, provide spaces large enough for customers to fill them in easily.

Don't forget your store name and address. Check every ad to be certain you have included your store name, correct address, telephone number, and store hours. Even if yours is a long-established store, this is important. Don't overemphasize your signature, but make it plain. In a large ad, mention the store name several times in the copy.

Don't be too clever. Many people distrust cleverness in advertising, just as they distrust salespeople who are too glib. Headlines and copy generally are far more effective when they are straightforward. Clever or tricky headlines and copy often are misunderstood.

Don't use unusual or difficult words Many of your customers may not understand words familiar to you. Trade and technical terms, may be confusing and misunderstood. Everyone understands simple language. Nobody resents it. Use it.

Don't generalize. Be specific at all times. Shoppers want all the facts before they buy. Facts sell more.

Don't make excessive claims. The surest way to loose customers is to make claims in your advertising that you can't back up in your store. Go easy with superlatives and unbelievable values. Remember: If you claim your prices are unbelievable your readers are likely to agree.

Plan ad size carefully. Ad attention increases with the size of the ad.

SECTION TWO

We go step by step

Layout instructions
were developed by
Marianne Browning
Newspaper Ad Designer

When creating a visual ad there are a few things to remember

1st..... SIZE and FORMAT........
Use a consistent size and format in your ads. People reading the newspaper tend to scan ads. In any ad you have about four seconds to catch the readers eye. Consequently your ad must be recognizable even before their eyes zoom in on the copy. The goal is for people to say 'Oh, there is a Wild Bird Store ad!".

As you see, the ad to the right is rather large. For ease in explaining advertising it is the size I have chosen. Your ads could be larger or smaller. Just remember that a consistent size and format is important. This provides consistency.

2nd..... HEADER — — — — —

You will want to use a header. It is a good idea for the header to remain consistent through the ad campaign. The picture of the Red-winged Blackbird and the word Spring are the header for this series. For the Summer series the picture and text will change. The key is consistent eye catcher for the reader to pick up on.

Spring

Spring

3rd..... LOGO

The next thing I did was to place the Logo. Remember to leave room underneath for your address, hours, telephone number, etc.

What I also did was to create a **'friendly little hook'**. We want people to know that we are not just out to get their money we also want to get to know them. They are not just clients they are friends.

We would be glad to help you
Come and Visit

Your Logo and/or
store name, address
Phone, etc. etc

Spring

4th ..... LEAD IN · · · · · · · · · · · · · · ·

Birds begin their migration north now

Once we have grabbed the readers eye, their attention will zoom into the ad and will focus onto the copy.

I decided to put in a nice little lead in line to create a pleasant mood for the reader. If you decide to do this make the type style (font) light and airy. I have put this line in italics. No special reason just personal taste. This line, while its text may change, will remain in the same place throughout the series of ads.

We would be glad to help you Come and Visit

Your Logo and/or store name, address Phone, etc. etc.

Spring

Birds begin their migration north now

Join the fun watching Birds at the Feeder

5th ..... HEADLINE

This line is important because it is our 'Headline'. This is the point we are running the ad. We are working to get the customer to consider our proposal. Your 'Headline' should be direct and to the point.

Remember consistency. The text may change but the position of the 'Headline" will remain in the same place throughout the ad campaign.

We would be glad
to help you
Come in and Visit

Your Logo and/or
store name, address
Phone, etc. etc

6th ..... COPY

Lastly we add the **why**. What brings the customer into your Wild Bird Store. What exactly is it that we are trying to sell them.

At this point you can decide whether or not you want to feature a specific product, price, promotion and/or a visual (picture).

I went with general copy and a visual. As before the copy and picture will change with each ad, but the positioning will not.

Spring

Birds begin their migration north now

Join the fun watching Birds at the Feeder

Your Copy
should answer

Product
Promotion
Price
Place
The call to
  action

We would be glad
to help you
Come in and Visit

Your Logo and/or
store name, address
Phone, etc. etc

REMEMBER:

... Consistency
... Cleanness
... Clarity

Zoom their eye into your ad
Grab their attention
Make your point
Call your customer to action

Published by
NAIWBS
Author
John Gardner
4317 Elm Tree Road
Bloomfield NY 14460

Advertising Notes

Samples of Ads that have worked:

Marketing Brief

The Series:

1. Gearing up for Greater Sales

150 pages of help during times when things need a boost.
Available from Amazon

2. Fall and Winter Wild Bird Feed Sale

Based on 41 years of experience in holding wild bird feed
sales - Available from Amazon

3. Newspaper Advertising Workbook

Don't start advertising until after you read this manual.
Scheduled Publication in Early March 2016

4. Location, Location, Location

How the big boys do it.
Pending Publication in Mid-March 2016

5. The Wilkerson Formula

How to make $9,000 on a weekend
Pending Publication near the end of March 2016

www.ingramcontent.com/pod-product-compliance
Lightning Source LLC
Chambersburg PA
CBHW070802180526
45168CB00004B/1726